Octopuses
For Kids

Amazing Animal Books
For Young Readers

By
Rachel Smith

Mendon Cottage Books
JD-Biz Corp Publishing

Read More Amazing Animal Books

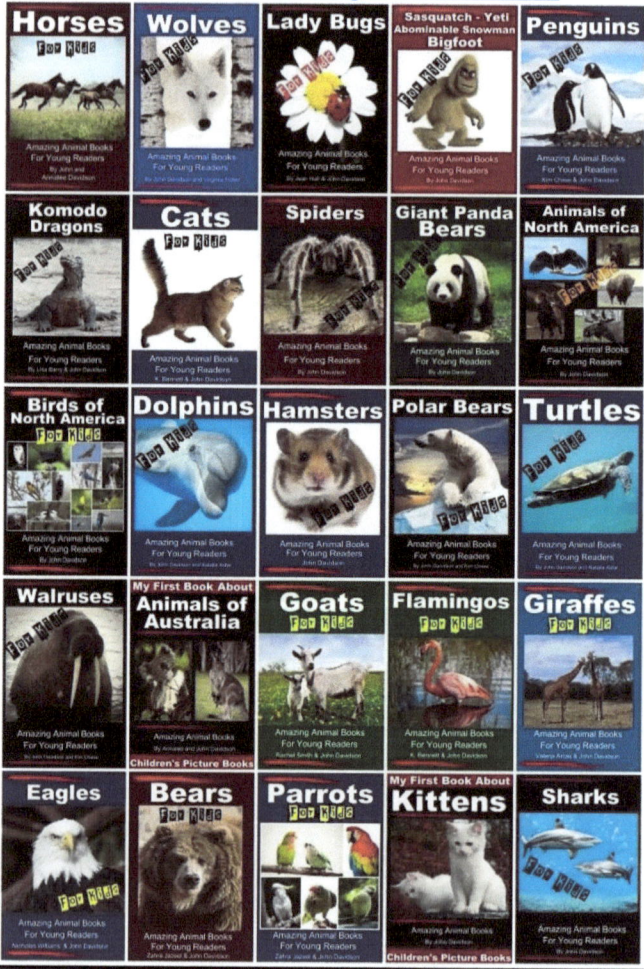

Purchase at Amazon.com

Table of Contents

Introduction

The octopus has long fascinated the human mind. They and their relatives are called 'cephalopods' which literally means 'head-foot' in Ancient Greek. The octopus has appeared on several vases and other items in Ancient Greek artifacts.

The Ainu people (who are a minority in Japan) have a great octopus , called Akkorokamui, which is said to be bright red and possibly glowing. This creature has been made a minor god in Shintoism, and is worshiped by some Japanese people.

A more modern octopus was an octopus named Paul. People believed he could predict soccer tournaments, and he was highly prized. He died a little while back.

Lastly, the Hawaiian people's creation myth involves the octopus: they say that the world has been remade several times, and since the last time, only the octopus survived from the old world, an alien among newer creations.

The octopus inspires interest wherever it is. Soon, you will see why this creature is so amazing.

What are octopuses?

Octopuses are members of the order Octopoda. They belong to the group of cephalopods. It's a very different creature from many animals on the land, such as lions, rats, or lizards, but not that unusual for the ocean.

A giant pacific octopus.

Contrary to popular belief, octopus is not pluralized (made to refer to more than one) by changing it to the word 'octopi.' Octopi would work if octopus was a Latin word, but it is not. Instead, it is an Ancient

Greek-based word, and the right pluralization is either octopuses, which is more common, or octopodes.

Octopuses have eight limbs, called arms. They are different from their cousins the cuttlefish and the squid's feeding tentacles. They are covered in little suction cups that are excellent at sticking to things, though they never stick to each other; you don't want an octopus sticking to you, because they will often leave behind marks.

An octopus is fairly unique from other animals, in that its body contains no bones of any kind. The only hard substance in the octopus's body is the beak, which is in the center of its arms. That is made of chitin, a substance that is also in some beetle's wings.

However, it is only cirrate octopuses that have no bones or shells. Incirrate octopuses have two fins and a soft shell, and this means they can't fit into as small spaces as their fellow octopuses. This is fine for them, because they live in the deep, dark ocean, whereas cirrates live in reefs and other spots that they can hide in.

This means that they can fit into seemingly impossible places; at many aquariums and other places that house octopuses, they have been known to escape from seemingly completely secure places.

An octopus has great problem-solving skills. They'd been known to be able to free themselves from closed jars, escape from their exhibits and eat other animals, and to open test containers with food in them.

Octopuses don't live very long; they may live up to six months, in many cases. However, some of the larger octopuses may live to be five years old. The issue that usually ends an octopus's life is mating; a female dies about a month after, and a male a few months after. The only way an octopus lives to be something like five years old is because they haven't mated.

They also have three hearts: two for their gills, and one for the rest of the body. Octopuses don't need air, but they do need oxygen, which is in both the air and the water; their gills separate the oxygen from the water to survive.

How do octopuses live?

Octopuses are not highly social creatures; they're not like wolves, who live in packs, or bees, who live in huge numbers together. Instead, the octopuses typically come together when they mate.

A common octopus.

An octopus moves in several ways. One way is through crawling; this means they use their arms to move along the ocean floor. Another way is through swimming, head first and arms dragging behind. They also do jet propulsion, which is more typically done when in danger.

When the octopus is threatened, it will often let out a cloud of ink, and then swim away as fast as it can.

However, its biggest defense is camouflage. Octopuses generally prefer to hide or run than to fight, but some have been known to take down sharks in a fight.

There's one other thing octopuses can do, when threatened with a predator: like some lizards, their arm will come free when a predator grabs onto it. It will continue to move and react to the predators attack, and it often distracts the predator so the octopus can get away. The arm will grow back, just like a lizard's tail.

An octopus has several senses; it has great eyesight, which has been shown to be able to see color in some kinds of octopuses. They have two organs near their eyes that help them understand where their bodies are horizontally and sense their movements. They always have their pupils (the holes in their eyes that let in light) in a horizontal shape.

Octopuses have been shown to be incredibly intelligent, though it's very much debated among scientists how smart they are. They've been shown to have both short term and long term memory; short term memory is when they remember something that just happened for a short time. Long term memory is when they remember something for a long time, like adults who remember when they were children.

They also have been shown to be able to tell the difference between different shapes and patterns. They also use tools.

One thing that is very interesting about octopuses (and very different from humans) is that their arms are somewhat autonomous (which means they can move without direction from the brain). The directions that come from our brains must come only from our brains; an octopus's directions comes partly from its brain, partly from other parts of the nervous system.

Octopus reproduction is not that complicated; the mother carries the eggs, and the father fertilizes them. The mother then lays up to 20,000 eggs, and protects them from predators. The reason she dies about when the eggs is that she never leaves the eggs, not even to eat. She starves to death to bring new octopuses into the world.

What do octopuses eat?

It really depends on what kind of octopus it is. Octopuses vary distinctly based on where they live.

An octopus on a coral reef.

Some kinds of octopuses, who live on the bottom of the ocean, eat things like crabs and clams. Octopuses who live more in the open sea will eat things like prawns and fish, and even other cephalopods.

The way that octopuses eat is through using their venom. All octopuses have venom, though it's a very small number that can kill humans. This venom is generally paralyzing to its prey.

An octopus will inject the prey with the venom and then tear it into small pieces to put into its beak. When it's dealing with a hard-shelled creature, octopuses have been known to drill a hole in its shell and then inject them. They pull out the creature's soft body to eat after that.

Some octopuses have been known to fight, subdue, and eat some kinds of sharks. Sometimes, an octopus will even eat a seabird, if they get the opportunity.

Where do octopuses live?

Octopuses live in the ocean. This means they live in saltwater, rather than freshwater, habitats. You will not find a live octopus in a pond or a river.

A mimic octopus.

Unlike land animals, an octopus is not limited to one country or one continent. They live in almost every saltwater location, and have been seen by most seafaring peoples. In fact, the octopus is a popular food in some countries, though it's often described as rubbery.

As for more specific places where they live, the octopus can live in the deep, dark parts of the ocean as well as the shallows.

Deep, dark places in the ocean are places we know less about. This is partly due to the darkness, and partly due to the difficulty of the pressure that is there down near the bottom of the ocean. Many, many creatures still live in this area that we don't know about, and they're often somewhat translucent or transparent (which means they have see-through skin).

Octopuses that live on the bottom of the ocean, in the deep, dark parts, tend to be cirrina types of octopus.

However, there are also octopuses that live in the upper part of the ocean and in the shallows. These types of octopus tend to be brighter colors; some are blue, red, brownish, and all sorts of colors.

Octopuses that live in the shallows tend to be smaller, whereas octopuses out in the open ocean are bigger. We know a lot more about the octopuses in these areas than the deep ocean octopuses.

Cirrina versus Incirrina

There are two types of octopus , as was mentioned before. These two types are the cirrina and the incirrina. These names for the two types come from the word 'cilia.'

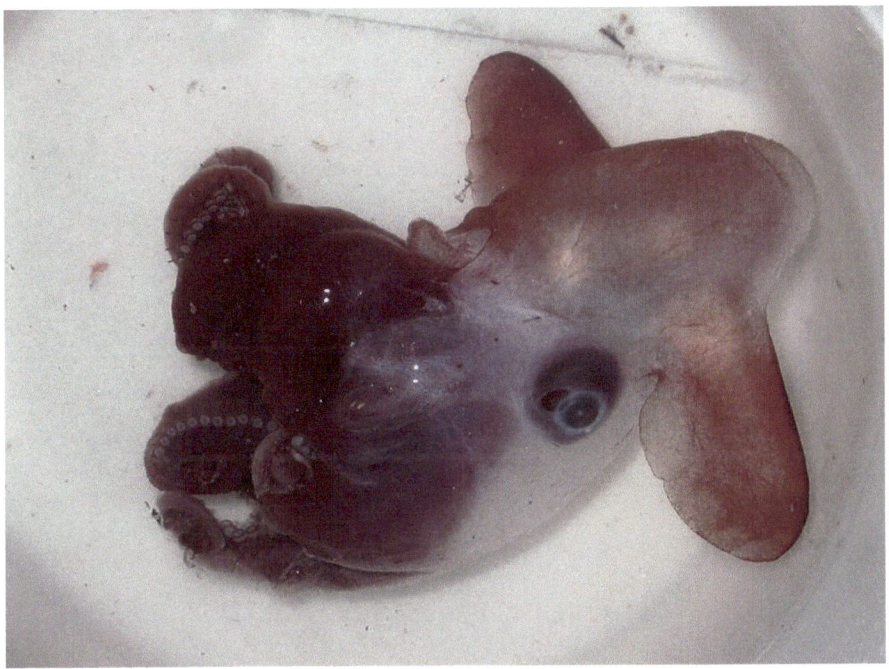

A cirrina octopus. Notice how it has fins on the sides of its head.
Picture Courtesy Wikipedia Commons

Cilia is a kind of wiggly part of a creature. Humans have really tiny cilia in their lungs, for example; they are used to move along mucus and such.

The cirrina octopuses have much bigger, though still fairly small, cilia. They have one of them on each side of their suckers. This makes them look a bit more alien than the octopuses that don't have them. Cirrina octopuses include umbrella octopuses, which have membranes between their arms so they look like an umbrella. Most cirrina octopuses have a soft shell, and two fins on the sides of their heads, as mentioned before.

Cirrina octopuses tend to live in the deep, dark ocean depths.

Incirrina, on the other hand, is the octopus most people are more familiar with. These are a lot of different kinds of octopus, because we can study them more since they aren't in the dark ocean depths.

Most incirrina octopuses look like the pictures in this book, but there are also gelatinous (goopy-looking) octopuses , and some with pretty short arms, among other kinds.

Some even look like they only have seven arms, though that is not the case. However, the key to incirrina octopuses is that they have no external (outisde) or internal (inside) skeleton of any kind, no shells or bones.

There are also glass octopuses in this group, with completely transparent flesh. You can see their insides. Otherwise, however, they are normal octopuses.

Blue-ringed octopuses

Blue-ringed octopuses are the only type of octopus venomous enough to kill a human. There are three (possibly four) types.

A blue-ringed octopus.

The biggest portion of these octopuses live around Australia; some, however, live as far North as Japan, and as far West as India.

They are beautiful; blue-ringed octopuses have, as you might've guessed, blue rings. They are easily recognizable by this. When they feel threatened, they turn yellow and their blue rings become startlingly bright.

Blue-ringed octopuses are actually very docile (calm and unthreatening) in behavior. They don't just attack people for no reason; usually, it's only when they're scared that they are any threat to humans.

They tend to hide most of the time. When they haven't turned bright colors, or when they purposely camouflage themselves, they blend in well. They also tend to live in small crevices, so that it's safe from predators.

Its venom is delivered through its bite. It paralyzes the animal, so they are easy to eat. However, it will also bite things that threaten it, not just its usual prey of crabs and shrimp; it's a small octopus, so it doesn't actually want to try to eat big animals like sharks and humans.

This type of octopus only lays fifty eggs, and the female keeps them warm under her arms. Like all octopuses, she dies of starvation about a month after the eggs are fertilized.

Common octopus

The common octopus is the one that most of the seafaring Western world know well. Its range is one of the largest, reaching from the Mediterranean Sea (where Italy and other countries are), to the North, to as far South as Senegal (which is an African country), and all the way across to North America.

A common octopus.

The common octopus is called Octopus Vulgaris. It is the only invertebrate (meaning, without a backbone) to be protected in scientific studies in the United Kingdom. This is because it is highly intelligent;

the proof is its raids of lobster traps and other things it figures out, such as escaping from its tank.

This kind of octopus prefers tropical, somewhat shallow waters. It's most likely to be found in the Mediterranean and other warmer places. Sometimes, when it's very hot out, it will go into deeper water than it normally does.

There are many different temperatures and levels of salinity (salt) in the water it lives in, though the common octopus does have preferences. It can't breathe through the top of the water, so it stays near the ocean bottom. It breathes through its skin and through gills that require a water intake, which means that time out of water is dangerous; however, it's not unusual for a common octopus to move in the open air for a short time.

For this octopus, swimming along is rare. This is because the jet propulsion (forcing water through their 'head') is a strain on the octopus's vessels and heart, and can't be done for very long.

Another thing that is cool about octopuses of this kind (and many other kinds): their temperature tends to be the same as the water they're in. This is why you don't generally see octopuses at the North Pole or Antarctica.

This octopus has arms that are each a meter long! It's popular as a food, especially in Africa. Its'head (and its mantle) is not as long as its limbs.

Paul the Octopus, mentioned in the beginning as the octopus who could predict who would win a tournament, was a common octopus.

Mimic octopus

The mimic octopus does what its name suggest: mimics, or looks like and pretends to be different species and such. It's the animal who wins the prize for most imitations.

A mimic octopus.

A mimic can change its skin color, and also its texture. It can pass itself off as a mossy rock or a lionfish. It's very unique in its ability to take on different shapes; no other animal goes quite so far as the mimic octopus.

This kind of octopus lives in the Indo-Pacific area, meaning near places like Indonesia, but it has been found in farther reaches than scientists originally thought it lived.

An octopus of this kind is naturally a brownish color, and very small. It is far smaller than the common octopus. It usually takes on stripes to confuse predators or make themselves look poisonous.

Instead of crawling along the bottom of the ocean, this octopus jets along by pushing water through its mantle. It is usually just above the bottom of the ocean, looking for good creatures to eat.

The interesting thing about the mimic octopus is that its imitations (or mimicry) of other animals isn't limited to protecting itself. A mimic octopus will also imitate prey disguised as the prey to get close. For example, they made pretend to be a crab to sneak up on a crab; the crab will think it's a suitor, and allow it close-- and then the octopus will eat the crab.

The mimic octopus is truly impressive in its mimic abilities. Pretty much every animal that mimics another animal, such as flies that mimic bees, only mimics one animal. No one knows for sure how many the mimic octopus can imitate, but there seems to be no limit.

Here are a few it can imitate:

Sea snakes. These types of snakes are venomous, and they are striped white and black. So the mimic octopus changes to that color and shows only two of its tentacles , pointed in different directions. Because the sea snakes are dangerous, it is left alone.

Lionfish. This is a spiny, poisonous fish. It is striped white and brown, and the mimic octopus will make its legs look like spines and the rest of its body appear to be the fish. No predators eat them, so if the mimic octopus looks like them, predators will avoid it.

Jellyfish. The mimic octopus will puff up its head and let its arms dangle. No animal wants to tangle with a jellyfish, since its venom is very dangerous. They tend to leave them alone, and that makes it the perfect animal for the mimic octopus to imitate.

Flatfish. A flatfish is a flat fish with both eyes on one side of its body. They camouflage well, and some smaller kinds are poisonous, which means that eating them could kill the predators who see them. Mimic octopuses will flatten themselves out and act like flatfish to sneak along the ocean floor.

While not animals, they will also imitate tube worm tubes and sponges that live in their area. Some places the mimic lives, it's a very dull, hard to hide in area. This means that when they want to move around, they will pretend to be colorful flounders, but otherwise they will stay quite well hidden.

What does the mimic octopus eat? Since its habitat is shallow and not all that great for large animals, it eats mostly small crustaceans (like little crabs) and small fish.

The mimic was not discovered in many of its habitats for a long time, due to its excellent hiding abilities.

Giant Pacific octopus

The giant Pacific octopus is considered to be the largest kind of octopus there is. There isn't complete agreement on this, though. Some think the seven-arm octopus might be bigger, or might be capable of getting bigger than the giant Pacific octopus. This has not been proved.

A giant Pacific octopus. This one is in an aquarium, and it's feeding time.

This kind of octopus lives in the Northern Pacific ocean; it lives near Korea, Russia, Alaska, and other such places. However, unlike a lot of the octopuses in this book, it lives in chilly depths. A giant Pacific octopus does better in the cold than its tropical neighbors, and it's a good thing, because it's very cold thousands of feet under water.

It can propel itself forward with jets like the common octopus, and it also squirts out ink to confuse predators. It has some webbing (skin and such) between its arms, so it often uses them to kind of parachute down onto prey.

The giant Pacific octopus is not too picky in what it eats; it will eat fish up to four feet in length, as well as sometimes attacking and eating small sharks. These are the ones that are best known for coming to the surface and attacking seabirds.

If it's protein, and within the range of size that this octopus could subdue it, it's likely they'll want to eat it. However, this octopus is not a danger to humans, because its venom will not kill humans, and they don't tend to be where humans are.

However, giant Pacific octopuses have predators. Sea otters, seals, and sperm whales all hunt the octopus. Humans also hunt the octopus, and people have been known to be able to catch them with their bare hands without injury.

Conclusion

There are many kinds of octopuses throughout the world. In English, they are called octopuses, octopi, and octopodes. However, whatever we call them, they will still be that strange, alien creature that makes us wonder what else is out there.

The octopus has been around for hundreds of millions of years, and it's great that we get to see them and learn about them by living in the same time era as them. We certainly don't see dinosaurs, or woolly mammoths. Octopuses are an amazing creature that might even end up being around longer than us.

Hopefully, it will be a very long time until then.

Author Bio

Rachel Smith is a young author who enjoys animals. Once, she had a rabbit who was very nervous, and chewed through her leash and tried to escape. She had pet fish, including a pink kissing gourami that liked to eat the other fish. She's also had several pet mice, who were the funniest little animals to watch. She lives in Ohio with her family and writes in her spare time.

Our books are available at
1. Amazon.com

2. Barnes and Noble

3. Itunes

4. Kobo

5. Smashwords

6. Google Play Books

Publisher

JD-Biz Corp

P O Box 374

Mendon, Utah 84325

http://www.jd-biz.com/

Mendon Cottage Books

P O Box 374, Mendon Utah 84325

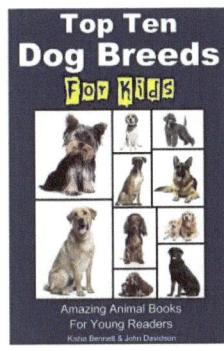

Top Ten
Dog Breeds
For Kids

Amazing Animal Books
For Young Readers
Katie Bennett & John Davidson

German Shepherds

Dog Books for Kids
K. Bennett

Bulldogs

Dog Books for Kids
K. Bennett

Dachshund

Dog Books for Kids
K. Bennett

Poodles

Dog Books for Kids
K. Bennett

Labrador Retrievers

Dog Books for Kids
K. Bennett

Rottweilers

Dog Books for Kids
K. Bennett

Boxers

Dog Books for Kids
K. Bennett

Golden Retrievers

Dog Books for Kids
K. Bennett

Puppies
Dog Books For Kids

AmazingAnimalBooks
By John Davidson

Beagles

Dog Books for Kids
K. Bennett

Yorkshire Terriers

Dog Books for Kids
K. Bennett

Dogs
Top Ten Dog Breeds
For Kids

Amazing Animal Books
For Young Readers
Zahra Jazeel & John Davidson

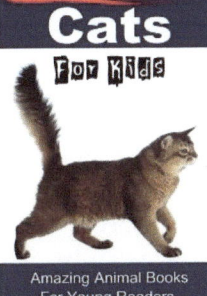

Cats
For Kids

Amazing Animal Books
For Young Readers
K. Bennett & John Davidson

Foxes
For Kids

Amazing Animal Books
For Young Readers
Zahra Jazeel & John Davidson

Wolves
For Kids

Amazing Animal Books
For Young Readers
By John Davidson and Virginia Fidler

www.ingramcontent.com/pod-product-compliance
Lightning Source LLC
Chambersburg PA
CBHW050908290526
45792CB00002B/745